Dear friend,

Never will I forget the time when a woman—a medical professional—began attending my evening Bible study. She was a smart, serious 30-year-old who was, at the same time, emotionally stuck. (Both of her parents had died of alcoholism at a relatively young age, a background that had caused her to feel adrift, somewhat floating in a sea of uncertainty.)

Immediately "Freda" responded to the wonderful scriptural truths and to our warm fellowship, much as a duck takes to water.

Two years later, Freda experienced a flood of sexual flashbacks—lewd, unnerving flashbacks that quickly increased with intensity. Late one evening as we talked, she described the graphic, disturbing scenes washing through her mind. Finally, she named the offender—her own father.

Freda became so frustrated—so full of anger—that she wanted to commit suicide. This was her statement: "Why live? I don't want to be alive any longer."

The more she focused on being a victim of incest, the more fragile she became. She couldn't read the Word. She couldn't hear the truth. She couldn't see the light. Although I rehearsed God's hope with her (hope she knew in her head), she had no hope for her heart. She said, "June, it will work for you, but it won't work for me." And she stopped taking part in our group.

Then one day I received a call from Presbyterian Hospital—the hospital where she worked—except this call was from the Psychiatric Unit. Freda had tried to commit suicide—and had almost succeeded. Freda had lost all hope.

Immediately, I went to the Psych Unit to have a heart-to-heart with her. "There are no hopeless situations," I said, "Only those who have grown hopeless. Freda, you have all the hope in the world—you have the God of hope indwelling you." Still she did not respond.

Eventually Freda's medical insurance ran out and she was sent to the state hospital. (Not good!) Two days later, I received a call, "June, you've got to get me out of here! These people here are like zombies. I'm not like these people."

Later in the conversation she said, "I've just been thinking. God does promise hope—and I can see that hope is for me. I can overcome this pain. I can do all things through Christ, who gives me strength." Interesting timing. I smiled.

Once Freda began focusing on the promises of God for herself personally, she improved dramatically. Within days she walked out of that asylum. As Freda was willing to work through the pain of the past, she began to walk in victory.

Let me share with you what I learned from Freda. When people need help, what is most important for them to receive? Truth, compassion, mercy? The most important of all is hope. Realize, even if they have truth in their heads, if they do not have hope that the truth will work, they can still walk away from your compassion and mercy and give up on life.

My prayer is that through this book, you will take hold of the hope God has for you so that you can live the life God has planned for you. The Lord says, "*I know the plans I have for you ... plans to prosper you and not to harm you, plans to give you hope and a future*" (Jeremiah 29:11). This means the Lord has a plan for your life, even amidst the pain.

When you put all the hurt into His hands, He will be your Healer, your Redeemer. And, ultimately, no pain is wasted.

Yours in the Lord's hope,

June Hunt

HOPE
The Anchor of Your Soul

The day is a cold January 25th. Two gale force storms have already shattered the main mast of the ship. In the third month at sea, a third terrifying storm, a "nor'easter," caused the Englishman to fear for his life—so much so, that he writes, "It was as if the great deep had already swallowed us up." Yet, on the same ship during the same storm, a group of German Christians appear completely calm as they quote the Psalms. According to young John Wesley, their lack of fear unsettled him more than the storm itself!

How can they be calm when their ship faces catastrophe? How can they be at peace when their lives are in peril? What makes their hope strong and his so weak?[1] All on the same battered ship, all weary from the same raging storm, all tossed by the same crashing waves—yet while one man feels frantic, the others keep calm. Why? Simply put: *Their lives were anchored in Christ, and they knew their anchor would hold.*

Some 150 years ago, these Mennonites, who clearly had a *peace that passes all understanding*, displayed their hope as though they were speaking directly to the Lord, *"When I am afraid, I will trust in you"* (Psalm 56:3). Not, *if* I am afraid, but *"When I am afraid, I will trust in you."*

What an anchor is to a ship, hope is to the soul. They both stabilize whatever needs to be held steady amidst the storms in life. Every Christian has been given a secure anchor in the person of Christ, for the Bible says about Jesus:

> **"We have this hope as an anchor**
> **for the soul, firm and secure."**
> **(Hebrews 6:19)**

DEFINITIONS OF HOPE

We have all been "in the same boat," with cloudy thinking about hope. The *common view* of hope in our culture is quite different from *Christian hope*. If you live by *cultural hope*, you will have a boatful of wishful thinking, and what you hope for will sometimes happen, and sometimes not.

However, *Christian hope* is based on the Bible—God's unchanging Word. By patiently relying on what God says, you will have all the hope necessary with all the certainty you will ever need. The apostle Paul states the source of our hope:

**"Everything that was written in the past
was written to teach us,
so that through endurance
and the encouragement of the Scriptures
we might have hope."
(Romans 15:4)**

When we live with biblical hope, we have an anchored life. We are held steady in the midst of any storm. Because hope is often misunderstood, an accurate understanding of the meaning of hope is crucial. The Bible says that when your hope is anchored in God, He will teach you His truth and lead you in the way you should go. This prayer is yours to claim:

> **"Guide me in your truth and teach me,**
> **for you are God my Savior,**
> **and my hope is in you all day long."**
> **(Psalm 25:5)**

▶ **Hope** identified as *cultural hope* is merely an *optimistic desire* that something will be fulfilled. This hope is not a guaranteed hope because it is subject to changeable people and circumstances.[2]

▶ **Hope** identified as *Christian hope* is an *optimistic assurance* that something will be fulfilled. This hope is a guaranteed hope not subject to change, but rather anchored in our unchangeable Savior and Lord.[3]

▶ **Hope** in the New Testament is conveyed by the Greek word *elpis*, which means a "favorable and confident expectation" relating to the future.[4]

Although the Bible uses the word *hope* in both the secular and the spiritual sense, the focus of our

Christian hope is always based on the *guaranteed* promises of God. Thus, this hope will never be a disappointment. As Christians, we are promised peace with God:

> **"We also rejoice in our sufferings,**
> **because we know that suffering produces**
> **perseverance; perseverance, character;**
> **and character, hope.**
> **And hope does not disappoint us,**
> **because God has poured out his love into**
> **our hearts by the Holy Spirit,**
> **whom he has given us."**
> **(Romans 5:3–5)**

WHAT IS Hopelessness?

When zealous religious leaders sought to kill the apostle Paul, he—a Roman citizen—appealed to Caesar. Soon Paul found himself a prisoner on a ship headed to Rome. A treacherous storm arose, and eventually all on board lost hope. All on board believed they would die. All on board saw the situation as *hopeless*. Paul admitted,

> **"When neither sun nor stars appeared for**
> **many days and the storm continued raging,**
> **we finally gave up all hope of being saved."**
> **(Acts 27:20)**

▶ **Hopelessness** is characterized by absolute despair with no expectation of good.[5] The Bible refers to those who have only a hope that perishes,

**"Such is the destiny of all who forget God;
so perishes the hope of the godless."
(Job 8:13)**

▶ **Hopelessness in the New Testament** is conveyed by the Greek word *apelpizo*, which is also translated "despair." (*Apo* means "away from" and *elpizo* means "to hope." When combined, this word literally means "to be away from hope.")[6]

▶ **Hopeless thinking** can result in a desire to die. Those who feel hopeless are unable to envision any viable option for their problems—death seems the only solution.

A ship without an anchor is vulnerable on the open seas—those aboard can lose hope of survival when a storm is severe. But, in the midst of our personal storms, rather than drowning in a sea of hopelessness, the Lord calls us to put our hope in Him, allowing Him to be our Anchor and relying on His promises. Let this be your personal prayer,

**"Sustain me according to your
promise, and I will live;
do not let my hopes be dashed."
(Psalm 119:116)**

For centuries, anchors have been a symbol of hope. This emblem was especially significant to the early persecuted church. Many etchings of anchors were discovered in the catacombs of Rome, where Christians held their meetings in hiding. Threatened with death because of their faith, these committed Christians used the anchor as a *disguised cross* and as a marker to guide the way to their secret meetings. Located beneath the ancient city, 600 miles of these tomb-like burial chambers served as a place of refuge during perilous times of persecution. Thus, the anchor—found even on some tombstones today—has become the symbol of guaranteed hope for the eternal security of true Christians. In the book of Proverbs, God, who is the Source of Wisdom, says ...

> **"Whoever listens to me will live in safety and be at ease, without fear of harm."**
> **(Proverbs 1:33)**

▶ **Anchors** are objects typically connected to a boat or ship by a long chain or a heavy line with a short chain for the purpose of holding a vessel in place. Some anchors are fastened securely to the water's flooring to hold down a large object (such as an oil rig). Other anchors are like large sheets or parachutes thrown into deep water in order to slow down or stabilize a vessel.

▶ **"Anchor,"** the English word, is a translation of a Greek word derived from *ankos*, which means "curve."[7] Anchors were usually curved so that they could hook onto a solid base.

▶ **Anchors** are a symbol of the sea and represent *hope* and *steadfastness*.

▶ **Anchors** are often Christian symbols representing Christ, who provides security for believers, holding them secure no matter the severity of the storm.

In Paul's terrifying time at sea, his ship encountered hurricane-strength winds, and the crew used not just one, but four anchors in an attempt to save both their ship and their lives.

> **"Fearing that we would be dashed against the rocks, they dropped four anchors from the stern and prayed for daylight."**
> **(Acts 27:29)**

Cultural hope is riddled through and through with the vacillating problems of our changing values, whereas *Christian hope* is woven through and through with the promises of our unchanging God. The Bible says,

> **"God is not a man, that he should lie, nor a son of man, that he should change his mind. Does he speak and then not act? Does he promise and not fulfill?" (Numbers 23:19)**

Cultural Hope Is Changeable

▶ Hope in society's values

PROBLEM: Your sense of right and wrong can slowly change over time. Social standards change as cultures change.

▶ Hope in legal justice

PROBLEM: Your sense of justice will not always be upheld. In legal courts, the *justice system* is *not always just*.

▶ Hope in people's promises

PROBLEM: Your faith can be fractured when people *break their promises*. People you look up to can let you down.

▶ Hope in an organization's integrity and rightness

PROBLEM: Your faith in any organization (even a church or ministry) can be destroyed as a result of *unrighteous behavior*—not doing what is right in God's sight—*a lack of integrity*.

▶ Hope in your education for wisdom and understanding

PROBLEM: Your education and the educational system do *not guarantee wisdom and understanding*. Wisdom is knowing how to apply your knowledge with godly insight.

▶ Hope in your work to provide purpose for your life

PROBLEM: Your work is not your purpose in life, nor is it your "identity," for *your work could come to an end*. Then, if you lost your work, you've just lost your purpose for living.

▶ Hope in your physical abilities

PROBLEM: Your physical body deteriorates with the passage of time so that you are *physically unable* to do all that you previously could do. Your body could become permanently disabled because of an accident or unexpected illness.

▶ Hope in your own financial provision

PROBLEM: Your plans can be *financially shattered* because of an economic or personal failure or crisis.

▶ Hope in your plans for the future

PROBLEM: Your *personal plans* for the future may be *unfulfilled*, for at any time your life could be cut short.

Christian Hope Is Unchangeable

▶ Hope in God's unchanging values

PROMISE: *"All your words are true; all your righteous laws are eternal. ... Great peace have they who love your law, and nothing can make them stumble."* (Psalm 119:160, 165)

▶ Hope in God's unchanging justice

PROMISE: *"He is the Rock, his works are perfect, and all his ways are just. A faithful God who does no wrong, upright and just is he."* (Deuteronomy 32:4)

▶ Hope in God's unchanging promises

PROMISE: *"If we are faithless, he will remain faithful, for he cannot disown himself."* (2 Timothy 2:13)

▶ Hope in God's unchanging integrity and righteousness

PROMISE: *"Your love, O LORD, reaches to the heavens, your faithfulness to the skies. Your righteousness is like the mighty mountains, your justice like the great deep. O LORD, you preserve both man and beast."* (Psalm 36:5–6)

► **Hope in God's unchanging wisdom and understanding**

PROMISE: *"He made the earth by his power; he founded the world by his wisdom and stretched out the heavens by his understanding."* (Jeremiah 51:15)

► **Hope in God's unchanging purpose for your life**

PROMISE: *"I cry out to God Most High, to God, who fulfills his purpose for me. ... For great is your love, reaching to the heavens; your faithfulness reaches to the skies."* (Psalm 57:2, 10)

► **Hope in God's unchanging abilities**

PROMISE: *"God is able to make all grace abound to you, so that in all things at all times, having all that you need, you will abound in every good work."* (2 Corinthians 9:8)

► **Hope in God's unchanging financial provision**

PROMISE: *"Command those who are rich in this present world not to be arrogant nor to put their hope in wealth, which is so uncertain, but to put their hope in God, who richly provides us with everything for our enjoyment."* (1 Timothy 6:17)

► **Hope in God's plans for your future**

PROMISE: *"So will it be with the resurrection of the dead. The body that is sown is perishable,*

it is raised imperishable ... it is sown a natural
body, it is raised a spiritual body. If there is a
natural body, there is also a spiritual body."
(1 Corinthians 15:42, 44)

QUESTION: "How can you be sure that
'Christian hope' is guaranteed and that God
will fulfill His promises?"

ANSWER: Christian hope can sound beyond
belief, unreal, far-fetched. For example, why
would anyone believe in God's promise of
the Christian's resurrection from the dead—a
permanent, physical resurrection—especially
since today we do not see people physically
resurrected? Nevertheless, you can have absolute
confidence in His hope *because of His character.*
When your life is yielded to the Lord, He promises
you a future filled with peace. He promises you
will live forever in His presence—and He does not
lie! The Bible gives this assurance: *"It is impossible
for God to lie"* (Hebrews 6:18).

WHAT IS the Difference between Faith and Hope?

Sometimes two words can be so intertwined
that it is difficult to distinguish between their
meanings. Such is the case with *faith* and *hope.*
Although aspects of the two overlap, the Bible
does differentiate between them. One of the most
famous verses in the Bible lists *faith* and *hope*

together with *love*. While most people think they understand love, they cannot clearly distinguish between faith and hope. Exploring the ways these two words are used in Scripture will shed light on both their uniqueness and similarity.

"These three remain: faith, hope and love. But the greatest of these is love." (1 Corinthians 13:13)

Differences between Faith and Hope

Hope is an assured promise, whereas *faith* is acting out that promise. Faith is hope put into action. Since "a picture is worth a thousand words," picture in your mind a ship anchored in the water.

▶ **The Water** represents a *sea of people* floating through life.

▶ **The Ship** in the water represents you *as a believer safe on board*.

▶ **The Anchor** in the water represents the guaranteed *hope that Christ will hold you secure* to keep you from drifting dangerously off course.

▶ **The Rode** is the strong chain where one end is connected to the ship and the other to the anchor. The rode represents an action—*acting in faith that Christ will hold you secure*. The act of "anchoring" (dropping the anchor and chain into the water) is based on the guaranteed *hope* that the anchor will hold.[8]

Having hope that we can be secure is necessary in order to be held secure. *Acting in faith* is necessary so that our hope is not merely a mental concept, but rather a living hope—a guaranteed hope that becomes a reality when we *experience* an anchored life.

► ***Our hope*** in Jesus is based on the promise of God. God the Father promised that God the Son would be the Savior of the world, thus our *hope* is Jesus.

   By faith we receive Jesus into our hearts and lives; therefore, faith is the means by which we actually receive our hope.

► ***Our hope*** in Jesus prompts us to step out in faith, taking God at His Word.

   Our faith is motivated by our hope, and faith is the means by which we benefit from our hope.

► ***Our hope*** for sustaining physical life resides in believing in the benefit of food (accepting the fact that eating food is necessary to stay alive).

   Our faith is exercised when we actually eat food for sustenance.

► ***Our hope*** for sustaining spiritual life resides in Jesus (accepting the fact that Jesus is necessary to have eternal life).

   Our faith in His ability to give us eternal life is exercised as we receive Jesus into our lives.

► ***Our hope*** for staying alive is our confident assurance in the merit of food; however, if we have no hope in the merit of food, we will not eat.

By faith, we eat food to stay alive, but by not eating, we will prematurely die.

▶ *Our hope* for eternal life is Jesus, but if we refuse to have hope in Him, we will die and spend eternity separated from Him.

Placing our faith in Christ is the means by which we take hold of our hope in Him and receive all the benefits of having Christ, including living throughout eternity in heaven with Him.

Christ has set you on His course, first to save you and then to conform you into His character. Having the assurance of hope is necessary before you can act in faith. Then, you act in faith because of your hope. Ultimately, the Bible says that your hope is the catalyst that produces your faith.

**"We have heard of your ... faith and love
that spring from the hope
that is stored up for you in heaven
and that you have already heard about
in the word of truth, the gospel."
(Colossians 1:4–5)**

Similarities between Hope and Faith

▶ Hope and faith are *integral to salvation*.

"In this hope we were saved. But hope that is seen is no hope at all. Who hopes for what he already has?" (Romans 8:24)

"It is by grace you have been saved, through faith—and this not from yourselves, it is the gift of God." (Ephesians 2:8)

▶ Hope and faith are *Christian virtues*.

"Since we belong to the day, let us be self-controlled, putting on faith and love as a breastplate, and the hope of salvation as a helmet." (1 Thessalonians 5:8)

▶ Hope and faith *involve the unseen*.

"In this hope we were saved. But hope that is seen is no hope at all. Who hopes for what he already has?" (Romans 8:24)

"We live by faith, not by sight." (2 Corinthians 5:7)

▶ Hope and faith *require trust*.

"May the God of hope fill you with all joy and peace as you trust in him, so that you may overflow with hope by the power of the Holy Spirit." (Romans 15:13)

"To the man who does not work but trusts God who justifies the wicked, his faith is credited as righteousness." (Romans 4:5)

▶ Hope and faith *please the Lord*.

"The LORD delights in those who fear him, who put their hope in his unfailing love." (Psalm 147:11)

"Without faith it is impossible to please God." (Hebrews 11:6)

The anchor of hope and the rode of faith can be seen as one. In boating, the rode is so securely connected to the ship and to the anchor that it can be considered "one" with them. This is the case in the Christian's relationship with Jesus Christ, our hope, our anchor. We have become one with Him, so that our *faith* and our *hope* are entwined like a braided rope—separate yet working as one, tethering us to our Lord. The Bible says ...

"Your faith and hope are in God."
(1 Peter 1:21)

CHARACTERISTICS OF MISPLACED HOPE

Anchors, which come in all sizes, shapes, and weights, are used to stabilize different objects in the water. When properly used, a relatively small anchor will successfully stabilize a large ship. For example, a 45-pound anchor can be used to stabilize a 4,000-pound ship.[9] Therefore, each anchor must be chosen based on the size and weight of the ship as well as on the anticipated weather and water bottom. Typically, ships set sail with different types of anchors onboard. Though terminology differs from place to place and from person to person, some have referred to three anchors as lunch, working, and storm anchors.

▶ The *lunch anchor* is dropped into the water of a bay to keep the ship in place for a short period of time.

▶ The *working anchor* is the ship's main anchor.

▶ The *storm anchors* (both bow and stern anchors) are put out when the ship encounters a severe storm.[10]

We all need a storm anchor for our lives, primarily because at different times we will be going into a storm or coming out of a storm or finding ourselves in the throes of a storm. When you have an anchored life—a life anchored in Christ—you cannot be destroyed by a tempestuous storm. The Lord will stabilize you until the storm has passed.

> **"When the storm has swept by,**
> **the wicked are gone,**
> **but the righteous stand firm forever."**
> **(Proverbs 10:25)**

WHAT ARE Inner Feelings of Hopelessness?

Have you ever felt a sense of hopelessness because you could not find a safe harbor for refuge? An anchor is constructed to stabilize a vessel in order to keep it from drifting into other vessels in a harbor or from capsizing in the turbulent waters of the sea.

We've all experienced that sinking feeling after our lives have drifted off course. Then we find ourselves in trouble, feeling emotionally overwhelmed. If we are not anchored in the promises of Christ, a catastrophic event could send us sinking into a sea of hopelessness. Our commitment should be this:

> **"Let us hold unswervingly to the hope**
> **we profess, for he who promised is faithful."**
> **(Hebrews 10:23)**

Do You Feel ...

▶ *Deceived?* Duped by someone you trusted

▶ *Disliked?* Deeming yourself unwanted by others

▶ *Dejected?* Dull, flat, and emotionally stuck

▶ *Deadened?* Dry, numb, and lifeless

▶ *Downcast?* Downhearted, assuming life will never change

▶ *Deprived?* Discriminated against with no chance to succeed

▶ *Disqualified?* Discounting that you have value

▶ *Degraded?* Demeaned and belittled by others

▶ *Detached?* Discarded by God and separated from others

▶ *Doomed?* Damned or trapped with no way out

QUESTION: "So many significant people have let me down. How can I live my life with any hope at all?"

ANSWER: Unquestionably, people fail people— all the more reason you need to put your hope in God, who will never fail you. He will be your unshakable rock and refuge.

"Find rest, O my soul, in God alone; my hope comes from him. He alone is my

rock and my salvation; he is my fortress,
I will not be shaken. My salvation and my
honor depend on God; he is my mighty rock,
my refuge." (Psalm 62:5–7)

WHAT ARE Outer Evidences of Hopelessness?

Have you ever felt that your life was shipwrecked? Being anchorless in a storm can cause a ship to capsize or crash onto the rocks. Likewise, being anchorless in life can cause you to careen into ruin. If you are living your life without the Lord as your security, you can find yourself shipwrecked—feeling disconnected, displaced, and distraught. For this reason you need to be ...

**"Holding on to faith and a good conscience.
Some have rejected these
and so have shipwrecked their faith."
(1 Timothy 1:19)**

Do You Look ...

▶ *Drained?* Drowning with exhaustion

▶ *Debilitated?* Depleted of energy and strength

▶ *Disinterested?* Drifting on a sea of apathy

▶ *Defeated?* Deadlocked from moving forward, feeling like a failure

▶ *Disgusted?* Down on life and pessimistic about living

▶ *Disconnected?* Divorced from meaningful people and meaningful purpose

▶ *Despondent?* Deteriorating in appearance and emotionally withdrawn

▶ *Displaced?* Desolate and lonely with no place to go

▶ *Distraught?* Driven to end dreams, end emotions, and end life

QUESTION: "I see no future for my life. How can I go on?"

ANSWER: You can go on because God purposefully created your life. He is always watching over you. And because of His unfailing love, you can always put your hope in the future He has planned for you.

> **"The eyes of the LORD**
> **are on those who fear him,**
> **on those whose hope**
> **is in his unfailing love."**
> **(Psalm 33:18)**

Does your life seem to be spiraling downward? If you are caught in a life-threatening storm, you feel a foreboding sense of doom—a frightening sense of despair.

If you've ever felt hopeless, it's as though you've become like a leaf caught in a whirlpool, spinning, spiraling downward, sucked inside the dark center. Those caught in this ominous vortex can feel the vexation of Jonah—disobedient Jonah, who rebelled against God and caused his own miserable plight.

> **"You hurled me into the deep,**
> **into the very heart of the seas,**
> **and the currents swirled about me;**
> **all your waves and breakers swept over me."**
> **(Jonah 2:3)**

Do You Have ...[11]

▶ *Disappointment?* Downcast with sadness over unfulfilled expectations

▶ *Doubt?* Distrust in yourself to do what is right

▶ *Discouragement?* Disheartened with no courage to risk again

▶ *Disillusionment?* Disenchanted with life because of broken promises

▶ *Depression?* Despondent with a heavy heart

▶ *Disdain?* Disgusted over too many wrong choices

▶ *Disunity?* Divided and confused within yourself

▶ *Disharmony?* Discord and continual disagreements with others

▶ *Despair?* Devastated with overwhelming helplessness

Drowning in Despair

Jonah was a man called by God to deliver a life-changing message of hope to an enemy nation. Instead, Jonah refused, rebelled, and ran to board a ship headed in the opposite direction. But because of his disobedience, the judgment of God fell upon the ship. Soon his shipmates threw him overboard. Jonah described this life-threatening situation and God's lifesaving intervention.

> **"The engulfing waters threatened me, the deep surrounded me; seaweed was wrapped around my head. To the roots of the mountains I sank down; the earth beneath barred me in forever.**
> **But you brought my life up from the pit, O Lord my God." (Jonah 2:5–6)**

Although Jonah temporarily obeys, his heart is filled with disdain for his enemies—even though *the entire city repents.* Later, overtaken with self-pity, he declares, *"I am angry enough to die"* (Jonah 4:9).

Unlike the anchorless person, if you have an anchored life, you will never drown in despair. An anchored life is not at the mercy of chance or circumstance. Swirling currents and pounding waves offer no cause for alarm when you abide in the One who is master over both the storms and the seas.

When you have Christ as your anchor, rather than drowning in despair, you are held secure with His hope. Imagine experiencing within minutes the extremes of both emotions—despair and hope. Imagine Jesus' apostles flailing about on a boat in the midst of a storm, fearing for their very lives. *How could He possibly sleep?* they wonder. Frantically, they call out to Jesus, *"Don't you care if we drown?"*

**"He got up, rebuked the wind
and said to the waves,
'Quiet! Be still!' Then the wind died down
and it was completely calm.
He said to his disciples,
'Why are you so afraid?
Do you still have no faith?'
They were terrified and asked each other,
'Who is this? Even the wind
and the waves obey him!'"
(Mark 4:39–41)**

Are You Harbored in Hope?

The disciples of Jesus experienced Him as their safe harbor. As long as they relied on Him, they had hope.

When you have Christ, you have ...

▶ *Contentment*—Being patient because of God's hope for you

"If we hope for what we do not yet have, we wait for it patiently." (Romans 8:25)

▶ *Courage*—Being bold because of God's hope within you

"Since we have such a hope, we are very bold." (2 Corinthians 3:12)

▶ *Confidence*—Being assured because of God's hope within you

"You have been my hope, O Sovereign LORD, my confidence since my youth." (Psalm 71:5)

▶ *Cheerfulness*—Being joyful because of God's hope for you

"Be joyful in hope, patient in affliction, faithful in prayer." (Romans 12:12)

▶ *Comfort*—Being encouraged because of God's unfailing love for you

"May your unfailing love rest upon us, O LORD, even as we put our hope in you." (Psalm 33:22)

▶ *Conviction*—Being anchored in hope because of God's Word within you

"May those who fear you rejoice when they see me, for I have put my hope in your word." (Psalm 119:74)

▶ *Christlikeness*—Being conformed to the character of Christ because of God's hope for you

"I eagerly expect and hope that I will in no way be ashamed, but will have sufficient courage so that now as always Christ will be exalted in my body, whether by life or by death." (Philippians 1:20)

Typically, ships at sea cannot survive the most severe storms without the use of anchors. And, if you are anchorless on the "sea of life," neither will you survive. However, as long as you have an anchored life, though battered and bruised, you will still be held secure. As long as you have an anchored life, you will weather the storms of life. Since there are many types of anchors, let's look at the following five.

Five Anchors for Any Condition

1 The Mushroom Anchor

- Mostly used for smaller vessels such as rowboats and canoes
- Least efficient as an anchor because it has no arms[12]

▶ *Jesus is our anchor.* As the mushroom anchor is used for smaller watercraft, Jesus stabilizes us as we move through the "smaller," more minor problems of everyday living. He helps us stay steady with people who gossip and gripe, who lie and are lazy, who pout and are petty, who annoy and are nosey. Jesus anchors us when we have frustrating friends, problems with pets, worry at work, and the list goes on.

BIBLICAL EXAMPLE: Some of the disciples of Jesus who were fishermen by trade experience the *frustration* of working all night, yet ended up empty-handed. Knowing this, Jesus tells them, *"'Put out into deep water, and let down the nets for a catch.' Simon answered, 'Master, we've worked hard all night and haven't caught anything. But because you say so, I will let down the nets'"* (Luke 5:4–5). Jesus then honors their obedience by filling their nets with more fish than they could possibly hold.

▶ *Jesus proves Himself to be our personal anchor* for the everyday trials of life.

"When they had done so, they caught such a large number of fish that their nets began to break. So they signaled their partners in the other boat to come and help them, and they came and filled both boats so full that they began to sink." (Luke 5:6–7)

2 The Fluke Anchor (e.g., the "Danforth Anchor")

- Lightweight, but with high holding power
- Buries into the water bottom, working best in sandy, muddy, or clay bottoms[13]

▶ *Jesus is our anchor.* Like the fluke anchor, Jesus stabilizes us with a powerful hold and a sense of peace. He is strong and steady, and yet His presence brings us peace—a "lightness" even in the heaviest of circumstances ... the death of a loved one, a devastating diagnosis. When we are struggling with ourselves and questioning our decisions, when we have unforeseen challenges and changes, when we are doubting who we are and doubting who He is, Jesus anchors us with His power and peace.

BIBLICAL EXAMPLE: Jesus sends the disciples ahead of Him by boat to the other side of the lake so that He can take time alone to pray. In the middle of the night Jesus walks toward the boat—on the water. Astonished, Peter instantly wants to join Jesus on the water. Jesus said, *"Come"*—and he does! He steps out, begins to walk, but then his faith in the known is weakened by the fear of the unknown. As he takes his eyes off Jesus, Peter is consumed with fear, starts to sink, and cries out. Then Jesus *reaches* out and rescues him.

▶ *Jesus proves Himself to be our personal anchor* when we look at life from our limited, finite point of view, rather than God's unlimited, infinite point of view, when doubt begins to dominate and faith begins to fail.

"'Lord, if it's you,' Peter replied, 'tell me to come to you on the water.' 'Come,' he said. Then Peter got down out of the boat, walked on the water and came toward Jesus. But when he saw the wind, he was afraid and, beginning to sink, cried out, 'Lord, save me!' Immediately Jesus reached

out his hand and caught him. 'You of little faith,'
he said, 'why did you doubt?' And when they
climbed into the boat, the wind died down."
(Matthew 14:28–32)

3 The Plow Anchor

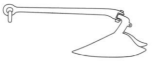

- Usually massive and heavy, often able to swivel

- Effective in rock, kelp, grass, weeds, sand, and mud (not in heavy grass)[14]

▶ *Jesus is our anchor.* Like the plow anchor, Jesus stabilizes us when all we can see all around us are problems. With its swivel capabilities, comes an agility and adeptness to anchor us through a variety of situations—poor choices, money problems, prodigal loved ones, painful losses. When our problems are perplexing, and what we see doesn't make sense, Jesus never fails to be our anchor.

BIBLICAL EXAMPLE: Immediately after Jesus miraculously feeds 5,000 men (plus women and children), He goes off alone to pray and sends His disciples by boat to Bethsaida. He knows they do not understand the meaning of the miracle. By evening the disciples reach the middle of the lake, struggling to paddle against the wind. Jesus watches them from the shore. Then in the late night hours, Jesus walks out on the lake. They become terrified, thinking they are seeing a ghost. Jesus quickly reassures them, climbs into the boat, and immediately the winds cease.

▶ *Jesus proves Himself to be our personal anchor* when we don't know how to think or what to do.

"When evening came, the boat was in the middle of the lake, and he was alone on land. He saw the disciples straining at the oars, because the wind was against them. About the fourth watch of the night he went out to them, walking on the lake. He was about to pass by them, but when they saw him walking on the lake, they thought he was a ghost. They cried out, because they all saw him and were terrified. Immediately he spoke to them and said, 'Take courage! It is I. Don't be afraid.' Then he climbed into the boat with them, and the wind died down. They were completely amazed, for they had not understood about the loaves; their hearts were hardened." (Mark 6:47–52)

4 The Claw Anchor

- Originally designed for offshore gas and oil rigs

- Most effective on rocky, gravel, and coral bottoms[15]

▶ *Jesus is our anchor.* Like the claw anchor, Jesus stabilizes us when we are victimized—when vehement verbal abuse, violence, or sexual abuse claws the heart and body—leaving us emotionally and spiritually scarred. For the times when we feel powerless, Jesus is our powerful anchor—holding us strong and secure.

BIBLICAL EXAMPLE: While inside a boat, Jesus tells His disciples that they will all go across to the other side of the lake. Once on the water, Jesus falls into a deep sleep and is not awakened by a storm that swamps the boat. The experienced crew believes they are sure to drown! In desperation they cry out to Jesus. With only a few words, He calms the storm, then questions their faith. After all, *hadn't He said* they were going across to the other side? *Didn't He imply* that they would indeed make it to the other side?

▶ *Jesus proves Himself to be our personal anchor* when the storms of life are so perilous that the thought of death seems imminent and the memory of His promises seems to fade.

"One day Jesus said to his disciples, 'Let's go over to the other side of the lake.' So they got into a boat and set out. As they sailed, he fell asleep. A squall came down on the lake, so that the boat was being swamped, and they were in great danger. The disciples went and woke him, saying,

'Master, Master, we're going to drown!' He got up and rebuked the wind and the raging waters; the storm subsided, and all was calm. 'Where is your faith?' he asked his disciples. In fear and amazement they asked one another, 'Who is this? He commands even the winds and the water, and they obey him.'" (Luke 8:22–25)

5 The Sea Anchor

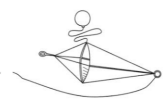

- Made of sturdy cloth like either a giant sail or a parachute

- Lowered into the water to create a drag and slow the vessel down, especially when the water depth is too great for other anchors to grab hold of the bottom

▶ *Jesus is our anchor.* Like the sea anchor, Jesus stabilizes us when we feel like a ship flailing in the water, tossed from side to side because of a compulsive addiction or besetting sin. In the depth of our souls, He slows us down, helping us to see how our continual wrong choices will wreck our relationships and shatter our dreams. Jesus anchors us when the powerful waves of personal disappointment leave us in despair—a hopeless state in which the only recourse seems to be death, anything to end the pain. Even in the most turbulent times, Jesus is there—He's our Anchor in the deep.

BIBLICAL EXAMPLE: Facing possible death, the prisoner Paul is being transported by ship to Rome to stand trial. In the midst of hurricane strength winds, the crew loses control of the ship. The tempestuous wind tosses the ship like a weightless cork toward the shore. In an attempt to diminish the speed, they let down the *sea anchor*. This is their only hope of not crashing into sandbars at a speed that would cause certain death.

▶ *Jesus proves Himself to be our personal anchor* when life hangs in the balance and all hope seems lost.

"*A wind of hurricane force, called the 'northeaster,' swept down from the island. The ship was caught by the storm and could not head into the wind; so we gave way to it and were driven along. ... When the men had hoisted it aboard, they passed ropes under the ship itself to hold it together. Fearing that they would run aground on the sandbars of Syrtis, they lowered the sea anchor and let the ship be driven along. ... When neither sun nor stars appeared for many days and the storm continued raging, we finally gave up all hope of being saved.*" (Acts 27:14–15, 17, 20)

When Jesus is your anchor, He can hold you secure in any storm because He has power over every storm.

CAUSES FOR MISPLACED HOPE TO FAIL

Have you ever had your hope fail? You cannot understand "*Why.*" You try to figure it out. You thought you had enough hope, plus a boat full of faith! Since the Bible says hope is the anchor for the soul, what causes an anchor to fail?

The problem could be that the anchor is the *wrong type* for the water bottom, or the *wrong size,* or the *wrong weight,* or made of a *wrong substance.* Or the *wrong technique* could have been applied, or the *wrong calculation* applied for the anchor rode—meaning too little, too much, or too weak, so that the holding power of the anchor is severely compromised.[16]

Many anchors that people rely on fail, causing hope to fail. In life, having the right anchor (hope) with the right rode (faith) is just as critical for the largest ocean liner as for the smallest boat. We all have placed our confidence in something or someone that did not hold or that broke under pressure.

Oh, the pain of placing all of our hope in a person, or in a position, or in (fill in the blank) only to discover that we have been terribly deceived. And what makes the deception worse is the fact that it was self-deception. Typically someone warned us—yet we failed to pay attention. Temporal "anchors," like possessions, popularity, power, or position were never designed to be our anchors for life. We are told, *"We fix our eyes not on what is seen, but on what is unseen. For what is seen is temporary, but what is unseen is eternal"* (2 Corinthians 4:18). What is temporary does not last. Jesus points out that misplaced hope fails because it is anchored in shifting sand:

"Everyone who hears these words of mine and does not put them into practice is like a foolish man who built his house on sand. The rain came down, the streams rose, and the winds blew and beat against that house, and it fell with a great crash." (Matthew 7:26–27)

Unreliable anchors cause devastating loss when they fail, and they inevitably do.

▶ Anchoring Our Hope in *Politics*

- Results in loss of hope when the political system crumbles

"The nations have fallen into the pit they have dug; their feet are caught in the net they have hidden." (Psalm 9:15)

45

▶ Anchoring Our Hope in *Economics*

- Results in loss of hope when resources of the economy weaken

"When times are good, be happy; but when times are bad, consider: God has made the one as well as the other. Therefore, a man cannot discover anything about his future." (Ecclesiastes 7:14)

▶ Anchoring Our Hope in *Society*

- Results in loss of hope when society rejects God's moral standard

"In those days Israel had no king; everyone did as he saw fit." (Judges 17:6)

▶ Anchoring Our Hope in *Law*

- Results in loss of hope when the legal system fails

"Do you rulers indeed speak justly? Do you judge uprightly among men? No, in your heart you devise injustice, and your hands mete out violence on the earth." (Psalm 58:1–2)

▶ Anchoring Our Hope in *Vocation*

- Results in loss of hope when work is not meaningful

"There was a man all alone; he had neither son nor brother. There was no end to his toil, yet his eyes were not content with his wealth. 'For whom am I toiling,' he asked, 'and why am I depriving myself of enjoyment?' This too is meaningless—a miserable business!" (Ecclesiastes 4:8)

▶ Anchoring Our Hope in *Health*

- Results in loss of hope when the body deteriorates

"My back is filled with searing pain; there is no health in my body." (Psalm 38:7)

▶ Anchoring Our Hope in *Money*

- Results in loss of hope when circumstances cause a monetary loss

"Riches do not endure forever, and a crown is not secure for all generations." (Proverbs 27:24)

▶ Anchoring Our Hope in *Marriage*

- Results in loss of hope when a spouse is not faithful

"The Lord is acting as the witness between you and the wife of your youth, because you have broken faith with her, though she is your partner, the wife of your marriage covenant." (Malachi 2:14)

▶ Anchoring Our Hope in *Friendship*

- Results in loss of hope when a friend betrays a confidence

"Even my close friend, whom I trusted, he who shared my bread, has lifted up his heel against me." (Psalm 41:9)

▶ Anchoring Our Hope in *Children*

- Results in loss of hope when children bring great pain upon their parents

"A foolish son brings grief to his father and bitterness to the one who bore him." (Proverbs 17:25)

"Brother will betray brother to death, and a father his child; children will rebel against their parents and have them put to death." (Matthew 10:21)

▶ Anchoring Our Hope in *Longevity*

- Results in loss of hope when a precious loved one dies

"There is a time for everything, and a season for every activity under heaven: a time to be born and a time to die, a time to plant and a time to uproot." (Ecclesiastes 3:1–2)

▶ Anchoring Our Hope in *Religion*

- Results in loss of hope when we glory in our good deeds rather than in God's gift of grace

"Be careful not to do your 'acts of righteousness' before men, to be seen by them. If you do, you will have no reward from your Father in heaven. ... And when you pray, do not be like the hypocrites, for they love to pray standing in the synagogues and on the street corners to be seen by men. I tell you the truth, they have received their reward in full." (Matthew 6:1, 5)

In 1912, the most magnificent ship ever built set sail on its maiden voyage. Heralded to the world as "unsinkable," how then could the *Titanic* sink? A total of 1,573[17] went to their watery graves because the owner of the shipping line failed to provide the needed lifeboats. He wanted to set a trans-Atlantic record for speed. The typical question people ask is, "*Why would God allow such a catastrophe?*" And typically, God gets the blame—even though the ship received warning after warning about icebergs.

Where is hope when God allows bad things to happen? Can you have absolute hope that "God's will" is going to prevail? What happens to your hope when "it" (what you are hoping for) doesn't happen? Some people get angry at God, others get angry with church, others get angry with life when their expectations are not fulfilled when "it" doesn't happen. What do we need to know about the will of God?

The Will of God

Surely it could not be *God's will* that so many people die in a shipwreck. So what happened to God's will? Three words can be used to describe the "will of God"—*perfect*, *permissive*, and *prevailing*.

▶ **God's *perfect* will**

- God has an ideal plan.

- God's plan is pleasing and good.

"Do not conform any longer to the pattern of this world, but be transformed by the renewing of your mind. Then you will be able to test and approve what God's will is—his good, pleasing and perfect will." (Romans 12:2)

EXAMPLE: God's perfect will is that everyone repent of sin and that no one perishes.

"The Lord is not slow in keeping his promise, as some understand slowness. He is patient with you, not wanting anyone to perish, but everyone to come to repentance." (2 Peter 3:9)

▶ **God's *permissive* will**

- God permits each person to exercise free will in opposition to His perfect will.

- God created people not as robots with no ability to choose, but as humans with the ability to choose independently of God.

"Choose for yourselves this day whom you will serve. ... But as for me and my household, we will serve the Lord." (Joshua 24:15)

EXAMPLE: God's permissive will is that everyone has the option of choosing right or wrong, spiritual life or spiritual death, being blessed or being cursed.

"This day I call heaven and earth as witnesses against you that I have set before you life and death, blessings and curses. Now choose life, so that you and your children may live." (Deuteronomy 30:19)

▶ **God's *prevailing* will**

- God's plans cannot be thwarted.
- God's ultimate purposes are achieved because He is sovereign.

"Many are the plans in a man's heart, but it is the Lord's purpose that prevails." (Proverbs 19:21)

EXAMPLE: God's prevailing will is to grant full forgiveness and a home in heaven to all who repent of their sins and trust in Jesus Christ as their Lord and Savior.

"I know that you can do all things; no plan of yours can be thwarted." (Job 42:2)

▶ Painful Circumstances

- "Since God ordains marriage and hates divorce, I'm believing God for the restoration of my marriage. He has to answer my prayers to reunite my family!"

- "I am certain that God will change my rebellious son because that would be in God's will."

- "I am confident that (<u>"it"—you fill in the blank</u>) *will* happen because that is what the Bible says *should* happen."

Conclusion: God indeed has His perfect will—however, He also gives people free will by allowing each of us to go against His perfect will. The "hope" you are given by God is not based on other people or circumstances. Your "certain hope" is that, regardless of the choices other people make and regardless of the severity of the storms in your life, if you choose to do His will, He will work out His purposes for you and ultimately give you peace that passes all understanding.

"Do not be anxious about anything, but in everything, by prayer and petition, with thanksgiving, present your requests to God. And the peace of God, which transcends all understanding, will guard your hearts and your minds in Christ Jesus." (Philippians 4:6–7)

Many people do not understand why their hope fails, yet in reality, their concept of hope is wrong. Consequently, understanding what *Christian hope* is and is not is most valuable.

Christian Hope Is ...

▶ *Not* dependent on another person or a group of people, but rather is dependent on the Lord alone

▶ *Not* wishful thinking, vague longing, or trying to fulfill a dream, but rather is assured, unchangeable, and absolute

▶ *Not* determined by circumstances, events, or abilities, but rather is determined by what is already secure and promised

▶ *Not* merely a desire, but rather is delayed fulfillment of reality

▶ *Not* dependent on the stars, luck, chance, or timing, but rather is predestined and settled in the heart and mind of God

"In him we were also chosen, having been predestined according to the plan of him who works out everything in conformity with the purpose of his will."
(Ephesians 1:11)

QUESTION: "Why is it so hard to have hope?"

ANSWER: Most people live by the saying: "Seeing is believing." If hope is so good, we want to see it, touch it, hold it. This mind-set is anything but new. After the Crucifixion, a certain apostle often called "doubting Thomas" refuses to have hope that Jesus had been seen alive. He declares to the other disciples, *"Unless I see the nail marks in his hands and put my finger where the nails were, and put my hand into his side, I will not believe it."*

A week later the *resurrected* Jesus stuns "Thomas the doubter" by showing him the holes in His hands and the scar in His side. From this moment on, he doubts no more. The skeptic becomes a believer saying to Jesus, *"My Lord and my God!"* Jesus responded, *"Because you have seen me, you have believed; blessed are those who have not seen and yet have believed"* (John 20:25–29).

Have you found yourself drifting through life? You know your life lacks direction, but you don't know what to do? Consider the "*Why.*" An unanchored ship in the midst of a storm drifts wherever the winds and waves carry it. Even in fair weather, a ship will drift just as aimlessly unless it has a captain to give it direction. Just as a ship needs an anchor to keep from drifting into other ships, we need an anchor to protect us from drifting into *destructive relationships.* Since many people are not only anchorless but also directionless in life, they are in need of a *captain* to provide direction and an *anchor* to provide security. Christians have both an anchor and a captain in Christ. The Bible says ...

> **"We must pay more careful attention,**
> **therefore, to what we have heard,**
> **so that we do not drift away."**
> **(Hebrews 2:1)**

1 The Winds of Fear

How do you survive the storms in life that severely threaten your moorings? What keeps your head above water when your heart is drowning? The way you navigate the dark nights of your soul says more about your faith in God than does the way you face your fair weather days.

"I know God can do anything; however, I'm really terrified that if I were to lose something that is dear to me such as my job or my health, there won't be anyone to take care of me."

► The Captain's view:

"The Lord himself goes before you and will be with you; he will never leave you nor forsake you. Do not be afraid; do not be discouraged." (Deuteronomy 31:8)

2 The Waves of Isolation

► Our viewpoint:

"I feel so lonely and isolated. I feel cut off from everyone—even from God."

► The Captain's view:

"When you pass through the waters, I will be with you; and when you pass through the rivers, they will not sweep over you. When you walk through the fire, you will not be burned; the flames will not set you ablaze." (Isaiah 43:2)

3 The Winds of Disbelief

► Our viewpoint:

"How can I believe in Christ when I don't see Him doing anything in my life?"

► The Captain's view:

"The one who calls you is faithful and he will do it." (1 Thessalonians 5:24)

4 The Waves of Persecution

▶ Our viewpoint:

"So many Christians are persecuted in the world. I don't understand how God could allow Christians to be killed."

▶ The Captain's view:

"Jesus said ... 'I am the resurrection and the life. He who believes in me will live, even though he dies.'" (John 11:25)

5 The Winds of Disillusionment

▶ Our viewpoint:

"I just knew that God was going to grant physical healing—but He didn't. I feel that God lied to me."

▶ The Captain's view:

"Who has known the mind of the Lord? Or who has been his counselor?" (Romans 11:34)

"God is not a man, that he should lie, nor a son of man, that he should change his mind. Does he speak and then not act? Does he promise and not fulfill?" (Numbers 23:19)

6 The Waves of Temptation

▶ Our viewpoint:

"No matter how hard I try, I am not able to achieve victory over this temptation. I don't understand why God won't help me."

▶ The Captain's view:

"No temptation has seized you except what is common to man. And God is faithful; he will not let you be tempted beyond what you can bear. But when you are tempted, he will also provide a way out so that you can stand up under it." (1 Corinthians 10:13)

WHAT IS the Root Cause of Hopelessness?

The famous Russian author Fyodor Dostoyevsky expressed the heartrending despair of hopelessness when he penned these well-known words:

To live without hope is to cease to live.
Hell is hopelessness.
It is no accident that above the entrance to
Dante's hell is the inscription:
"Leave behind all hope, you who enter here."[18]

No human being or situation can fulfill all your deepest needs. Both people and situations change throughout our lives. You may have days of feeling satisfied, but the satisfaction is temporary, the glimmer of hope fleeting. Only God can provide you with the love, significance, and security for which your heart longs.[19] And God stands ready to meet your deepest inner needs. This is His promise to you.

**"My God will meet all your needs
according to his glorious riches
in Christ Jesus."
(Philippians 4:19)**

▶ WRONG BELIEF:

"Nothing is meeting my real needs, and I have no reason to believe that will ever change. The future offers no hope for me."

▶ RIGHT BELIEF:

"I refuse to base my hope on anything that can be taken away from me. My hope is in my unchanging relationship with Jesus, my Lord and Savior. He is my Need-Meeter. In Him I have found the love, significance, and security that I need to embrace this life and to anticipate my future life in heaven."[20]

**"The LORD is good to those whose hope
is in him, to the one who seeks him."
(Lamentations 3:25)**

Life with Christ is endless hope. Without Him, it's a hopeless end.

Hopelessness: How to Have a "Forever Hope"

The Bible says that those who do not entrust themselves to Jesus will ultimately face an eternity of hopelessness. God promises heaven for all who believe. And to those who do not, He promises an eternity in hell, separated from all that is good. Dante described hell as being full of woe, pain, and loss ... and without hope. [21]

The good news is that God desires that you spend eternity with Him and to live your life through Him right now. He will give you hope that lasts forever—a hope found only in a secure relationship with Him.

How to Have Hope That Lasts Forever

#1 God's Purpose for You is *Salvation.*

What was the Father's motive in sending Jesus Christ to earth?

To save you through the fullest expression of His love!

"God so loved the world that he gave his one and only Son, that whoever believes in him shall not perish but have eternal life. For God

did not send his Son into the world to condemn the world, but to save the world through him." (John 3:16–17)

What was Jesus' purpose in coming to earth?

To forgive your sins, empower you to have victory over sin, and enable you to live a fulfilled life!

"I [Jesus] have come that they may have life, and have it to the full." (John 10:10)

#2 Your Problem is *Sin.*

What exactly is sin?

Sin is living *independently* of God's standard—knowing what is right, but failing to do what is right.

"Anyone, then, who knows the good he ought to do and doesn't do it, sins." (James 4:17)

What is the major consequence of sin?

Sin produces death, both spiritual and physical separation from God.

"The wages of sin is death, but the gift of God is eternal life in Christ Jesus our Lord." (Romans 6:23)

#3 God's Provision for You is the *Savior.*

Can anything remove the penalty for sin?

Yes! Jesus died on the cross to personally pay the penalty for your sins.

"God demonstrates his own love for us in this: While we were still sinners, Christ died for us." (Romans 5:8)

What is the solution to being separated from God?

Trust in the person of Jesus Christ as being God in the flesh and in His death and resurrection as providing the only way to God the Father.

"If you confess with your mouth, 'Jesus is Lord,' and believe in your heart that God raised him from the dead, you will be saved." (Romans 10:9)

#4 Your Part is *Surrender.*

Place your faith in (rely on) Jesus Christ as your personal Lord and Savior and reject your "good works" as a means of gaining God's approval.

"It is by grace you have been saved, through faith—and this not from yourselves, it is the gift of God—not by works, so that no one can boast." (Ephesians 2:8–9)

Receive the blessings of being God's child and of the Spirit. The moment you trust in Jesus— He gives you His Spirit to live inside you.

"You received the Spirit of sonship. ... The Spirit himself testifies with our spirit that we are God's children." (Romans 8:15–16)

Then the Spirit of Christ enables you to live the fulfilled life God has planned for you, and He gives you His peace and His hope for the future. If you want to be fully forgiven by God—and become the person God created you to be, you can tell Him in a simple, heartfelt prayer like this:

PRAYER OF SALVATION

God, I want a real relationship with You.
I admit that many times I've failed
to go Your way and instead
chosen to go my own way.
Please forgive me for my sins.
Jesus, thank You for dying on the cross
to pay the penalty for my sins
and for rising from the dead to provide new
life. Come into my life to be my Lord and
my Savior.
Place Your hope in my heart
and teach me to put my confidence in You.
Make me the person You created me to be.
In Your holy name I pray. Amen.

What Can You Expect Now?

After placing your trust in the completed work of Jesus Christ, look at what God says!

"Those who hope in the LORD will renew their strength. They will sore on wings like eagles; they will run and not grow weary, they will walk and not be faint."
(Isaiah 40:31)

STEPS TO SOLUTION FOR REGAINING HOPE

In ancient times, ships would have a "forerunner" (Greek: *proderomos*—"who went before us") known as the "anchorarius." This forerunner was in charge of the ship's main anchor. With a group of sailors, he would carry the anchor by means of a smaller boat into a safe harbor and set it there. Although the ship remained outside the harbor, it was anchored within and held secure against the wind and waves that would otherwise carry it out to sea or dash it against rocks along the shoreline.

The "forerunner" was the one person chosen to arrive at a designated place before others in the group—arriving first for three purposes:

▶ to give notice of their approach

▶ to take possession in their name

▶ to prepare for their arrival[22]

As your forerunner, Christ is your steadfast hope, anchoring you within the safe harbor of heaven (*"the inner sanctuary behind the curtain"*). He secures you here on earth and assures you of your eventual safe arrival there.

> **"We have this hope as an anchor
> for the soul, firm and secure.
> It enters the inner sanctuary
> behind the curtain,**

where Jesus, who went before us,
has entered on our behalf.
He has become a high priest forever, in the
order of Melchizedek."
(Hebrews 6:19–20)

Key Verse to Memorize

To regain a hopeful outlook on life is not difficult or complicated. All it requires is a shift in focus. The challenge comes in focusing not on "the storm" but on the hope God has for you when you are tossed by the storm. Because of God's faithfulness, *hope anchored in His character* will hold. That is why meditating on God's unfailing promises found in His unchanging Word will supply all the stability you will ever need.

"'I know the plans I have for you,'
declares the LORD, 'plans to prosper you
and not to harm you, plans to give you hope
and a future.'" (Jeremiah 29:11)

Key Passage to Read and Reread

The deepest failures in your life cannot thwart God's faithfulness to you. Do you know the genuine goodness of God in your life—His immense mercy, His constant compassion, His everlasting love? He will be faithful to you forever. Do you know how to experience such a hope that will anchor you through any storm? The Bible says to put your *hope* in Him. Repeatedly say when you are in the midst of the storm, *"I will **hope** in him"* (Lamentations 3:24 ESV).

**Lamentations 3:19–25: How to Put Your Hope
in Him**

▶ **Look** at the situation accurately.

*"I remember my affliction and my wandering,
the bitterness and the gall. I well remember them,
and my soul is downcast within me."* (vv. 19–20)

▶ **Line** up your thinking with what gives you
hope.

"This I call to mind and therefore I have hope."
(v. 21)

▶ **Learn** what gives hope in the midst of this
situation.

*"Because of the LORD's great love we are not
consumed, for his compassions never fail."* (v. 22)

▶ **Linger** on this fact: Every day God will be
faithful to you.

*"They are new every morning; great is your
faithfulness."* (v. 23)

▶ **Let** the Lord fulfill you totally—not just
partially.

*"The LORD is my portion; therefore I will wait
for him."* (v. 24)

▶ **Lean** on this truth to receive hope for your
heart.

*"The LORD is good to those whose hope is in him,
to the one who seeks him."* (v. 25)

Are you unable to make headway in your life? No matter what you do, your effort to move forward is thwarted—often you feel pushed backward. Such is the struggle when sailing with guilt. Imagine being in a small boat in the midst of a storm—but your guilt has caused holes in the hull. You try to move forward toward the safe harbor, but the strong winds hold you back.

Again and again, you bail out water, but you cannot bail fast enough. Finally, you tire out and give up. In severe exhaustion, you lose hope. The storm you could endure, but not with the *holes in the hull*.

When unable to make progress because of the storm gales of guilt, you need to discern the absolute truth about your guilt. Only by dealing with the truth can you plug the holes in the hull.

Discerning the Truth When Drowning in Guilt

▶ ***True Guilt*** is the result of having committed wrong.

- We need to "own" our guilt by taking personal responsibility for our part in the negative consequences that occur in our own lives or in the lives of others. Guilty feelings are designed by God to bring a sense of remorse over our wrong choices.

- Because our lives are to reflect God in all that we do, we naturally experience feelings of guilt over our past or present sins.

- This kind of personal guilt is actually "good guilt," designed by God to turn us around so that we will be what He created us to be and therefore do what He created us to do.

▶ *False Guilt* is the feeling of unjustified self-condemnation.

- This bad guilt is seen as being overly self-judgmental, overly responsible, overly conscientious, or overly sensitive when you have done no wrong or when you have repented and turned away from your wrong.

- This unhealthy guilt may be the result of having other people put you on a "guilt trip."

- False guilt can also be the impetus for extreme self-denial demonstrated by overly serving others (being a "people-pleaser"), low self-worth, and emotional blocks that produce negativity and hopelessness.

When guilt immobilizes you, the following steps will help you discern false guilt, thus allowing your heart to embrace the God of all hope.

**"You will know the truth,
and the truth will set you free."
(John 8:32)**

► **Discern the truth by honestly asking ...**

- "Do I have true guilt or false guilt?"

- "Have I truly repented of my sin, yet still live with guilt?"

- "Why am I struggling with hopelessness?"

- "Am I in any way responsible for my lack of hope?"

- "In what way does my guilt make my feelings of hopelessness worse?"

- "If my guilt were removed, would I feel hopeless?"

> **"If our hearts do not condemn us,
> we have confidence before God."
> (1 John 3:21)**

► **Once you discern the truth about your guilt ...**

- Sincerely ask God to forgive you for any true guilt that you are experiencing.

- Steadfastly place your hope in Jesus, choosing to believe in His personal acceptance of you.

- Saturate your mind with Scriptures that encourage you to receive God's complete acceptance of you.

> **"There is now no condemnation
> for those who are in Christ Jesus."
> (Romans 8:1)**

All of us experience deep grief and mourning. If you stay locked in a prison of emotional pain, your heart will become deadened to hope. Realize that you have a Savior who experienced the most severe grief—the One who agonized in the garden of Gethsemane with the anguish of His soul— Jesus, who said, *"My soul is overwhelmed with sorrow to the point of death"* (Matthew 26:38).

To Weather the Storm Gales of Grief ...

▶ Remember that some grief and suffering is natural and must be endured for a time.

"We do not lose heart. Though outwardly we are wasting away, yet inwardly we are being renewed day by day. For our light and momentary troubles are achieving for us an eternal glory that far outweighs them all." (2 Corinthians 4:16–17)

▶ Reach out to God with your grief and sorrow.

"The LORD is close to the brokenhearted and saves those who are crushed in spirit." (Psalm 34:18)

▶ Realize that Jesus has already borne for you all your grief and sorrow.

"He took up our infirmities and carried our sorrows, yet we considered him stricken by God, smitten by him, and afflicted." (Isaiah 53:4)

▶ Repent of any true guilt you may be experiencing.

"Godly sorrow brings repentance that leads to salvation and leaves no regret, but worldly sorrow brings death." (2 Corinthians 7:10)

▶ Reflect on fond memories of the past and allow yourself to grieve over specific events.

"There is a time for everything … a time to weep and a time to laugh, a time to mourn and a time to dance." (Ecclesiastes 3:1, 4)

▶ Reach out to a friend and share your pain.

"Carry each other's burdens, and in this way you will fulfill the law of Christ." (Galatians 6:2)

▶ Remain hopeful, knowing that this feeling of deep grief will pass.

"I tell you the truth, you will weep and mourn while the world rejoices. You will grieve, but your grief will turn to joy." (John 16:20)

▶ Reinforce your faith by giving hope to others.

"Praise be to the God and Father of our Lord Jesus Christ, the Father of compassion and the God of all comfort, who comforts us in all our troubles, so that we can comfort those in any trouble with the comfort we ourselves have received from God." (2 Corinthians 1:3–4)

Bitterness can be like a winter storm blowing in from the north. At first the signs are subtle, but soon bitterness swirls into a blizzard of complaints, unforgiveness, depression, sustained grief, hopelessness, and rage against God. Most people have great difficulty admitting that they are bitter. They say words like "I'm not bitter, but I just can't forgive him!" or "I'm not angry, but it's just not fair." Bitterness is buried anger that has become frozen in resentment. Like a chain that ties us to the past, we carry unresolved anger in our hearts wherever we go.

> **"See to it that no one
> misses the grace of God
> and that no bitter root grows up
> to cause trouble and defile many."**
> **(Hebrews 12:15)**

If You Are Struggling with the Biting Winds of Bitterness …

▶ Believe that it is possible, with God's help, to get rid of all of your resentment.

▶ Know that you are not a helpless victim of other people, circumstances, or events.

▶ Take personal responsibility for your attitude of bitterness.

▶ Confess before God that you are harboring anger. Express your true desire to overcome the bondage of bitterness.

▶ Search your heart for the past events or people that embitter your heart, then release your right for revenge.

▶ Understand that only a close relationship with Jesus can give you the love and confidence to let go. Leave your vengeance to the judgment of God.

▶ Cultivate a heart of forgiveness toward others that allows you to experience God's total forgiveness of you.

▶ Exercise faith in the promised hope that God will walk with you out of bondage into the light of a changed life.

"Hope does not disappoint us, because God has poured out his love into our hearts by the Holy Spirit, whom he has given us." (Romans 5:5)

He was 38 years old when he fed the dogs, went to the park, put a gun to his head, and committed suicide. Living with his mother, a lifeline for him during his recurring bouts with manic depression, he felt her imminent death from cancer was the death of all hope for him.

Jason had been a successful doctor with a brilliant career ahead, yet the dark storm clouds of his illness rained grief on his soul, dampened his thinking, and drowned his love for life. Due to his infidelity, his beautiful wife divorced him. Though he was treated for depression, Jason's rapid mood swings hindered the effectiveness of medications.

This particular storm had ripped his confidence to shreds and swept away his sense of control, thus leaving him feeling helpless. Being stripped of self-reliance and harboring no hope for a better future, Jason, along with many others like him, saw no way out of the storm, so he ended his life. If only he had grasped the hope that God held out to him in the midst of his storm, he might have developed a different perspective and made a different choice.

> **"There is surely a future hope for you, and your hope will not be cut off." (Proverbs 23:18)**

If You Are Seeking to Help Someone Find Hope in the Midst of a Life-threatening Storm ...

▶ Don't think you can "do it all," but encourage the person to talk with you by expressing concern and empathy. Severe depression is usually characterized by a withdrawn state of mind and a reluctance to share feelings. Acknowledge the reality of deep pain and suffering. Be supportive, and encourage the person to pursue medical treatment. Explain that medical help and therapies are available and are very successful.

▶ Suggest that the person fight suicidal thoughts by engaging in certain activities that could help.

- Keep a journal and write down your thoughts throughout the day.

- Go out often with friends and family, even if you have to push yourself to do so.

- Develop awareness of your thoughts and feelings in order to recognize when suicidal thoughts might be coming on.

- Read one Psalm every morning and one every night before going to sleep.

▶ Talk about suicide with the person. Talking about it does not plant the idea in someone's head. Talking actually provides an opportunity to explore thoughts, feelings, and reactions. Again, provide affirmation and assurance.

▶ Ask direct questions regarding the existence of a plan. Ask how, when, and where in order to gain valuable information to help prevent an attempt. Do not promise confidentiality if this is the case.

▶ Encourage the person to go to professionals to seek testing and therapy. Work with these professionals and keep them and the person's doctor and therapist completely informed. Keep a list of all the numbers you will need to call in case there is an emergency.

▶ Ask for a signed contract that obligates the suicidal person to talk with you or with someone else before taking harmful action. "Will you promise that you will first call me if you are considering harming/killing yourself?" Write the words out like a contract and both of you sign and date it.

▶ Take care of yourself physically, emotionally, and spiritually. You may begin to feel stress and feelings of depression when working with a person who is suicidal. Ask others for help, and stay as close to your own normal routine as possible.

▶ If there is a crisis, call 911 immediately!

**"A wise man's heart guides his mouth,
and his lips promote instruction.
Pleasant words are a honeycomb,
sweet to the soul and healing to the bones."
(Proverbs 16:23–24)**

In a novel by Daniel Defoe, Robinson Crusoe was shipwrecked on a desolate isle. He alone survived while everyone else on board drowned. Though separated from humanity, he did not starve. Though without clothes, in the hot climate he didn't need them. Though he was on an island with no supplies, since his ship was wrecked near the shore, he could get all necessary items. He concluded that no situation was so miserable that something good couldn't come from it. No matter the "bad," there was something to be thankful for. When we find ourselves shipwrecked in life, we have a choice about our attitude—and a choice as to what we will do. We are to put our hope in the Lord and thank Him for how He will use our trials.

"Give thanks in all circumstances, for this is God's will for you in Christ Jesus." (1 Thessalonians 5:18)

Consider This ...

Reality is not merely what you see—it is what God says![23]

IF YOU SAY: "I've lost hope."

GOD SAYS: Hold on to My hope.

"Find rest, O my soul, in God alone; my hope comes from him." (Psalm 62:5)

IF YOU SAY: "It's impossible."

GOD SAYS: All things are possible with Me.

"What is impossible with men is possible with God." (Luke 18:27)

IF YOU SAY: "I cannot do it."

GOD SAYS: You can do all things through Christ.

"I can do everything through him who gives me strength." (Philippians 4:13)

IF YOU SAY: "I'm not able to do what I need to do."

GOD SAYS: I am able to give you all that you need.

"God is able to make all grace abound to you, so that in all things at all times, having all that you need, you will abound in every good work." (2 Corinthians 9:8)

IF YOU SAY: "Nothing good can come from this."

GOD SAYS: I know how to bring good out of this.

"We know that in all things God works for the good of those who love him, who have been called according to his purpose." (Romans 8:28)

IF YOU SAY: "I can't meet all my needs."

GOD SAYS: I can meet all your needs.

"My God will meet all your needs according to his glorious riches in Christ Jesus." (Philippians 4:19)

IF YOU SAY: "I don't know the way."

GOD SAYS: I'll teach you My way.

"He guides the humble in what is right and teaches them his way." (Psalm 25:9)

DRIFTING: How to Have an Anchored Life

While certain companies only build anchors, other companies only test anchors. Each new anchor is taken out on a ship, attached to a chain, and cast overboard. The casting is repeated at different depths of water and into different water bottoms containing different sediments. Stress is put on the anchor to see if the metal or the shaft of the anchor will twist or break or if the flukes of the anchor will drag or slip. Each of the anchors is tested before it is sold in order to establish that it will hold secure.[24]

We have an anchor—Jesus—who, when tested, has never bent, broken, slid, or slipped. Therefore, when the stresses of life come your way, as your anchor, He will hold you firm and secure.

**"He lifted me out of the slimy pit,
out of the mud and mire;
he set my feet on a rock
and gave me a firm place to stand."
(Psalm 40:2)**

(The following is an acrostic on the word *ANCHOR*.)

A ccept Christ as your only hope.

> *"I pray also that the eyes of your heart may be enlightened in order that you may know the hope to which he has called you, the riches of his glorious inheritance in the saints, and his incomparably great power for us who believe. That power is like the working of his mighty strength, which he exerted in Christ when he raised him from the dead and seated him at his right hand in the heavenly realms."* (Ephesians 1:18–20)

N ever put your hope in what is seen, but hope in what you do not see.

> *"In this hope we were saved. But hope that is seen is no hope at all. Who hopes for what he already has? But if we hope for what we do not yet have, we wait for it patiently."* (Romans 8:24–25)

C laim the plans and promises of God.

> *"'I know the plans I have for you,' declares the LORD, 'plans to prosper you and not to harm you, plans to give you hope and a future.'"* (Jeremiah 29:11)

H ope in the redeeming power of God.

> *"Why are you downcast, O my soul? Why so disturbed within me? Put your hope in God, for*

I will yet praise him, my Savior and my God."
(Psalm 42:5)

O ffer genuine faith, hope, and love to other Christians.

"We always thank God, the Father of our Lord Jesus Christ, when we pray for you, because we have heard of your faith in Christ Jesus and of the love you have for all the saints—the faith and love that spring from the hope that is stored up for you in heaven and that you have already heard about in the word of truth, the gospel that has come to you. All over the world this gospel is bearing fruit and growing, just as it has been doing among you since the day you heard it and understood God's grace in all its truth."
(Colossians 1:3–6)

R each out to others so that they might know the hope of His calling.

"I pray also that the eyes of your heart may be enlightened in order that you may know the hope to which he has called you, the riches of his glorious inheritance in the saints, and his incomparably great power for us who believe. That power is like the working of his mighty strength." (Ephesians 1:18–19)

If you have ever sailed on a ship, did you actually take the time to express thanks for the anchor? Most people would never think to be thankful for so vital a piece of equipment. Likewise, have you ever genuinely thanked God for giving you hope? A certain hope, a guaranteed hope, an assured hope? This hope can never disappoint you.

Since the Bible says, "In all things give thanks," one way to thank God is to look at the descriptive words before the word *hope*. In the Bible, certain adjectives shed light on the meaning of our hope in Christ. They make hope come alive! They will help you focus on the relevance of hope in your life—especially when you are in the midst of a storm and need reassurance that you have an anchor that holds. The apostle Paul, who knew what it was like to lose hope, says to us,

> **"Let us hold unswervingly
> to the hope we profess,
> for he who promised is faithful."
> (Hebrews 10:23)**

Thanking the Lord for His different kinds of hope will not only be pleasing to Him, but also a blessing to you.

Based on the Bible, Thank God for Your ...

▶ **Living Hope**—"Thank You, Jesus, that You saved me from being spiritually dead in my sins and that I am now spiritually alive."

*"Praise be to the God and Father of our Lord Jesus Christ! In his great mercy he has given us new birth into a **living hope** through the resurrection of Jesus Christ from the dead."* (1 Peter 1:3)

▶ **Better Hope**—"Thank You, Jesus, for saving me from a legalistic way of living—thank You for setting me free!"

*"The former regulation is set aside because it was weak and useless (for the law made nothing perfect), and a **better hope** is introduced, by which we draw near to God."* (Hebrews 7:18–19)

▶ **One Hope**—"Thank You, Jesus, for calling me into a relationship with You, for the unity I now have with all true believers and for the one hope we all share because of You."

*"There is one body and one Spirit—just as you were called to **one hope** when you were called."* (Ephesians 4:4)

▶ **Good Hope**—"Thank You, Jesus, for Your love, and thank You for your grace. I thank You that You made it possible for me to have eternal encouragement because of all the good that You are storing up for me in the future."

*"May our Lord Jesus Christ himself and God our Father, who loved us and by his grace gave us eternal encouragement and **good hope**, encourage your hearts."* (2 Thessalonians 2:16)

▶ **Future Hope**—"Thank You, Jesus, that You have a future planned for me both here on earth and in heaven. And thank You that my future will not be cut short—it is dependent on You alone."

*"There is surely a **future hope** for you, and your hope will not be cut off."* (Proverbs 23:18)

▶ **Blessed Hope**—"Thank You, Jesus, for placing in my heart the exuberant anticipation of seeing You face to face when You appear again."

*"We wait for the **blessed hope**—the glorious appearing of our great God and Savior, Jesus Christ."* (Titus 2:13)

Why does the Lord ask you to put your hope in Him? Without a doubt, it is not for His sake, but for yours! Christ will keep you from being wrecked by the crushing events of life. You will be tossed about by the waves and battered by the winds, but your faith in Him can replace your fear. Although your anchor is unseen, you will feel its pull and know it is holding you. Realize, the stronger the storm, the stronger the pull. No matter what storm you might be presently enduring or what storm you might soon be encountering, if your anchor is Jesus Christ, your anchor will hold!

Extraordinary benefits await the one who holds on to His hope—benefits based on the promises of God—benefits both in this present life and in the life to come. Jesus would not have sacrificed *His life* if it would not have benefited *your life*. How humbling to realize that you cannot earn or deserve the benefits of hope—they are a gift of grace to you based on the Lord's great love for you.

**"Put your hope in the Lord,
for with the Lord is unfailing love and with
him is full redemption."
(Psalm 130:7)**

The Benefits of Hope

When you feel uncertain about life, adrift on an uncharted course, the Lord wants you to look to Him as your anchor and to rely on His compass—His biblical promises—to chart your course. Jesus supernaturally fed 5,000, walked on water, healed the sick, calmed the storm, raised the dead, and performed many other miracles. Since Jesus is God, if He is your anchor, He will hold you secure and fulfill every promise.

His Blessed Hope ...

▶ **Provides you joy in living**

"Be joyful in hope, patient in affliction, faithful in prayer." (Romans 12:12)

▶ **Generates faith and love in you**

"We have heard of your faith in Christ Jesus and of the love you have for all the saints—the faith and love that spring from the hope that is stored up for you in heaven and that you have already heard about in the word of truth, the gospel." (Colossians 1:4–5)

▶ **Causes you to live a pure life**

"Everyone who has this hope in him purifies himself, just as he is pure." (1 John 3:3)

▶ **Inspires you to persevere with endurance**

"We continually remember before our God and Father your work produced by faith, your labor prompted by love, and your endurance

inspired by hope in our Lord Jesus Christ."
(1 Thessalonians 1:3)

▶ Uplifts your downcast soul

"Why are you downcast, O my soul? Why so disturbed within me? Put your hope in God, for I will yet praise him, my Savior and my God."
(Psalm 42:5)

▶ Causes you to praise God

"As for me, I will always have hope; I will praise you more and more." (Psalm 71:14)

▶ Anchors your soul

"We have this hope as an anchor for the soul, firm and secure. It enters the inner sanctuary behind the curtain." (Hebrews 6:19)

▶ Generates boldness in you

"Since we have such a hope, we are very bold."
(2 Corinthians 3:12)

▶ Develops your patience

"If we hope for what we do not yet have, we wait for it patiently." (Romans 8:25)

▶ Gives you reason to rejoice

"Through whom we have gained access by faith into this grace in which we now stand. And we rejoice in the hope of the glory of God."
(Romans 5:2)

▶ Establishes your security and safety

> *"You will be secure, because there is hope; you will look about you and take your rest in safety."* (Job 11:18)

▶ Guarantees your eternal life

> *"He saved us, not because of righteous things we had done, but because of his mercy. He saved us through the washing of rebirth and renewal by the Holy Spirit, whom he poured out on us generously through Jesus Christ our Savior, so that, having been justified by his grace, we might become heirs having the* **hope of eternal life***."* (Titus 3:5–7)

Although seagoing vessels require *three or more anchors,* in Christ *a Christian has an "all-purpose" Anchor,* who has taken hold of heaven for us and secures us there and, at the same time, holds us secure through every situation here. When He was tested, He was victorious over the most violent of storms. He withstood the ferocious winds the army of hell sent against Him. He was strong enough to withstand the heaviest stress without breaking. His holding power is without question. The strong rode that connects the believer to Him is saving faith. When you are securely connected to Jesus through faith, you receive salvation and are guaranteed a priceless destination—a paradise—a place called heaven.

> "We have put our hope in the living God,
> who is the Savior of all men,
> and especially of those who believe."
> (1 Timothy 4:10)

Conclusion: *Your Anchor Holds.*

Hundreds of classic hymns contain lines, verses, and choruses describing Jesus as our anchor, our hope, our stay. Such is the hymn "The Solid Rock." Read slowly the lines and take to heart the truths that will indeed give hope to your heart.

THE SOLID ROCK

*My **hope** is built on nothing less*
Than Jesus' blood and righteousness;
I dare not trust the sweetest frame,
But wholly lean on Jesus' name.

When darkness veils His lovely face,
I rest on His unchanging grace;
In every high and stormy gale
***My anchor holds** within the veil.*

His oath, His covenant, His blood,
Support me in the whelming flood;
When all around my soul gives way,
*He then is all **my hope and stay**.*

Refrain:
On Christ, the solid Rock, I stand;
All other ground is sinking sand,
All other ground is sinking sand.[25]

SCRIPTURES TO MEMORIZE

Whom should I be **seeking** to meet my needs?

*"The LORD is good to those whose hope is in him, to the one who **seeks** him."* (Lamentations 3:25)

How can I **plan** for the **future** when the present seems so hopeless?

*"'For I know the **plans** I have for you,' declares the LORD, 'plans to prosper you and not to harm you, plans to give you hope and a **future**.'"* (Jeremiah 29:11)

How can I **hope** to get over the **shame** of my past?

*"No one whose **hope** is in you will ever be put to **shame**, but they will be put to shame who are treacherous without excuse."* (Psalm 25:3)

Why do I still feel so dissatisfied when I have accumulated so much **wealth**?

*"Command those who are rich in this present world not to be arrogant nor to put their hope in **wealth**, which is so uncertain, but to put their hope in God, who richly provides us with everything for our enjoyment."* (1 Timothy 6:17)

What I have **looked for** in life is gone. How can I have any **hope**?

*"But now, Lord, what do I **look for**? My **hope** is in you."* (Psalm 39:7)

When my heart is **downcast** and **disturbed**, what am I to do to regain **hope**?

> *"Why are you **downcast**, O my soul? Why so **disturbed** within me? Put your **hope** in God, for I will yet praise him, my Savior and my God."* (Psalm 42:5–6)

What proof do I have that **Christ** can give me **hope**?

> *"Praise be to the God and Father of our Lord Jesus **Christ**! In his great mercy he has given us new birth into a living **hope** through the resurrection of Jesus Christ from the dead."* (1 Peter 1:3)

Is anything in this life **unchangeable** and **secure**?

> *"Because God wanted to make the **unchanging** nature of his purpose very clear to the heirs of what was promised, he confirmed it with an oath. ... We have this hope as an anchor for the soul, firm and **secure**."* (Hebrews 6:17, 19)

How can I have **hope** in the midst of my **suffering**?

> *"We also rejoice in our **sufferings**, because we know that suffering produces perseverance; perseverance, character; and character, hope. And **hope** does not disappoint us, because God has poured out his love into our hearts by the Holy Spirit, whom he has given us."* (Romans 5:3–5)

What can I choose to **rejoice** about?

> *"We **rejoice** in the hope of the glory of God."* (Romans 5:2)

NOTES

1. George Sweeting and David Sweeting, The Acts of God (Chicago: Moody Press, 1986), 219.

2. *American Heritage Electronic Dictionary* (Houghton Mifflin, 1992), s.v. "Hope."

3. W. E. Vine, *Vine's Complete Expository Dictionary of Biblical Words*, electronic ed. (Nashville: Thomas Nelson, 1996), s.v. "Hope."

4. Vine, *Vine's Complete Expository Dictionary*, s.v. "Hope."

5. *Merriam-Webster Collegiate Dictionary* (2001); m-w. com, s.v. "Hope."

6. Vine, *Vine's Complete Expository Dictionary*, s.v. "Despair."

7. Vine, *Vine's Complete Expository Dictionary*, s.v. "Anchor."

8. Robert Jamieson, A. R. Fausset, and David Brown, *Commentary Critical and Explanatory on the Whole Bible* (1871), http://bible.crosswalk. com/Commentaries/JamiesonFaussetBrown/jfb. cgi?book=heb&chapter=006.

9. Solarnavigator, "Anchor History and Development," Solarnavigator, 2005, http://www.solarnavigator.net/ anchors.htm.

10. David Brown, "All About Anchors: A Complete Guide to Anchor Gear Selection," Boats.com, 1996, http://www.boats.com/boat-articles/ Anchoring+Equipment-100/All+About+Anchors/2179. html.

11. Geoff Gorsuch, "Caught In a Downward Spiral," *Discipleship Journal* 52 (1989): 19–20.

12. National Safe Boating Council, "Teach and Learn: Types of Anchors," Boatingsidekicks.com, 2001, http:// www.boatingsidekicks.com/TEACH/anchortypes.pdf.

13. Don Casey, "Anchoring," Boat Owners Association of the United States, 2006, http://www.boatus.com/boattech/anchorin.htm.

14. Casey, "Anchoring," http://www.boatus.com/boattech/anchorin.htm.

15. Casey, "Anchoring," http://www.boatus.com/boattech/anchorin.htm.

16. Casey, "Anchoring," http://www.boatus.com/boattech/anchorin.htm.

17. Chuck Anesi, "Titanic Disaster: Official Casualty Figures and Commentary," http://www.anesi.com/titanic.htm

18. Fyodor Dostoyevsky, in Marshall Shelley, *Helping Those Who Don't Want Help*, Leadership Library (Carol Stream, IL: CTI, 1986), 75.

19. Lawrence J. Crabb, Jr., *Understanding People: Deep Longings for Relationship*, Ministry Resources Library (Grand Rapids: Zondervan, 1987), 15–16; Robert S. McGee, *The Search for Significance*, 2nd ed. (Houston, TX: Rapha, 1990), 27–30.

20. Ibid.

21. Dante, Alighieri, "Inferno," The Divine Comedy, 3.1.9.

22. Theological Dictionary of the New Testament. Edited by Gerhard Kittel, Geoffrey William Bromiley and Gerhard Friedrich. electronic ed. (Grand Rapids, MI: Eerdmans, 1964-c1976).

23. David F. Burgess, Encyclopedia of Sermon Illustrations (St. Louis: Concordia Publishing House, 1988), 104.

24. Chuck Hawley and Tony Gasparich, "West Marine Sand Anchor Test," United States Sailing Association, 1994, http://www.ussailing.org/safety/Studies/1994sfanchortest1.htm.

25. Edward Mote, "The Solid Rock," in *Worship and Service Hymnal for Church, School, and Home* (Chicago: Hope, 1957), 293.

SELECTED BIBLIOGRAPHY

Aikman, David. *Hope: The Heart's Great Quest.* Ann Arbor, MI: Vine, 1995.

Crabb, Lawrence J., Jr. *Understanding People: Deep Longings for Relationship.* Ministry Resources Library. Grand Rapids: Zondervan, 1987.

Gorsuch, Geoff. "Caught In a Downward Spiral." *Discipleship Journal* 52 (1989): 19–20.

Hunt, June. *Seeing Yourself Through God's Eyes.* Eugene, OR; Harvest House Publishers, 2008.

MacIntosh, Mike. *The Tender Touch of God.* Eugene, OR: Harvest House, 1996.

McGee, Robert S. *The Search for Significance.* 2nd ed. Houston, TX: Rapha, 1990.

Morgan, Donald W. *How to Get It Together When Your World Is Coming Apart.* Old Tappan, NJ: Fleming H. Revell, 1988.

Patterson, Ben. *Waiting: Finding Hope When God Seems Silent.* Downers Grove, IL: InterVarsity, 1989.

Roush, H. L., Sr. *Jesus Loves Me.* Belpre, OH: H. L. Roush, Sr., 1978.

Shelley, Marshall. *Helping Those Who Don't Want Help.* Leadership Library. Carol Stream, IL: CTI, 1986.

West, Kari. *Dare to Trust Dare to Hope Again: Living with Losses of the Heart.* Colorado Springs, CO: Faithful Woman, 2002.